25 Gifts for Christmas

25 Gifts for Christmas

Turning Holiday Chaos into a Season of
Love, Healing, and Comfort

TATIANA 'TAJCI' CAMERON

To purchase additional copies of *25 Gifts for Christmas*, visit www.25GiftsForChristmas.com

Cover design and layout by Mark Daniel Studio

Cover photo of Tatiana by Marijana Marinovic

Interior art illustrations by Tatiana 'Tajci' Cameron

Page design and layout by T. Cameron

Visit www.WakingUpRevolution.com for more information about author/singer/life coach Tatiana 'Tajci' Cameron, and to learn more details about her upcoming musical performances, her group and one-on-one coaching, her online coaching programs, and various products available for sale.

Printed in the United States of America

ISBN-13: 978-1-9780-4575-0

First Edition: December 2017

10 9 8 7 6 5 4 3 2 1

To a fellow human of the Earth who moved to Mars in search of a calmer, more magical, and kinder Christmas.

You are missed.

(No kids were harmed in the process.)

:)

Contents

Preface

I grew up in Croatia (formerly a part of Yugoslavia), where we spent our Christmases quietly. It was a festive time, but not much, and certainly nothing like how it is celebrated in America.

All we had at home around Christmas time was a little Charlie Brown-like tree with a few old German ornaments hanging off of it. Only a few gifts carefully wrapped by my mom—maybe a pair of socks, a chocolate bar, or pencils from Italy—were underneath the tree.

After I moved to America, I cried every holiday season. At first it was from the wonder and joy I found in gorgeous decorations, beautiful music, the spirit, and the sacred story celebrated by so many people. Later, when I started having my own kids, the tears came from being overwhelmed and stressed out; sometimes, even disappointed. I couldn't understand why Christmas trees were thrown out the day after Christmas! For me, the holidays would begin on Christmas Eve and last for the full Twelve Days. I needed that time to soak in the magic, savor the peace, and honor the sacredness of this beautiful holiday. After all, I worked hard to prepare for the holidays.

One of my favorite American Christmas traditions is the Advent Calendar. I'd buy one for my sons every year. I absolutely loved watching them open tiny paper windows and finding a surprise. I'd watch them cherish each small gift and saying something like "Wow! I always wanted one of these!" Or "This one is the best yet!" Each of the 25 gifts surpassed the previous one, not because of its objective value, but because of my child's excitement and appreciation.

For years, I secretly hoped someone would gift me with an Advent Calendar. When I got tired of waiting, I made my own.

I hope you enjoy it!

SPECIAL INSTRUCTIONS

Readers of this book are encouraged to visit 25GiftsForChristmas.com, where the following bonus features are available with the purchase of this book:

1. Audio narrations of each of the 25 Gifts that can be downloaded and played back on personal devices at the reader's convenience.

2. A "Gratitude Tree" poster on which to write down, compile, and save gratitude statements explained with each of the 25 Gifts.

3. Audio downloads of Christmas/spiritual songs that accompany most of the 25 Gifts described in the book. A CD with the songs, all sung by the author, Tatiana 'Tajci' Cameron, is also available for a nominal cost plus shipping.

Introduction

Welcome! I'm grateful you are holding this book in your hands and reading these words.

I composed *25 Gifts for Christmas* with an old fashioned Advent Calendar in mind. The kind that reveals a surprise gift each day—a chocolate, or a rhyme! I offer it to you as a chance to bring peace, order, and TLC to yourself during an otherwise hectic time of the year—the twenty-five days of Advent leading up to Christmas. More than likely, you have been buying gifts and, on behalf of others, preparing to celebrate the holiday season and Christmas. Now it's time to bestow some of that spirit of giving on yourself!

That's right—here are twenty-five gifts just for you, one for each day of the Advent season!

I invite you to reserve some time just for yourself each day. The idea is to open these gifts mindfully, fully present in a moment made just for you. Perhaps you can do this in a quiet spot somewhere in your home. Or, if you live in a warmer climate, you can take each of these 25 Gifts outdoors with you via the accompanying audio downloads, available for you to listen to as you take your daily walk. You can take these gifts in and reflect on them, contemplating what each one brings to you. Then, each day, write down three things relating to each gift for which you are grateful.

Think back to any time you watched a child open a gift. Maybe it was on a Christmas morning or on their birthday. You probably noticed how so incredibly focused they were when tearing open the ribbon-bound wrappings, their eagerness about to turn into astonishment!

Nothing can distract them from that gift. And then, when they hold it in their hands, able to gaze at it, they either scream with joy or they stare at it with a sense of curiosity, deciding in their heads if they are going to play with it right away or wait until later. Maybe they still need to decide if they even like it.

Now, it's your turn—again—years later to get some gifts of your own and perhaps to relive some of that childhood awe and excitement as you get to enjoy being the recipient of your twenty-five daily gifts. That is the essence of *25 Gifts for Christmas*, and my wish for you this holiday season.

You can use use the downloadable Gratitude Tree on which to write down your three daily thoughts of gratitude. Think of it: by the end, you will have seventy-five instances of gratitude that will become your own permanent keepsake reminder of all that you have to be thankful for.

A bonus available to you, as a buyer of this book, is a playlist of Christmas songs. I hope you will enjoy them and that they will enrich your experience.

My prayer for you with this book and this Advent season is to accept and take each gift with that same childlike wonder from years past and embrace it as a gift for you and only you—the "you" on your inside who perhaps is a bit tired, worn out, and stressed about all that's going on in your life and in our world.

All right, let's begin!

P.S. If you are looking for gift ideas for your friends and family, visit www.25GiftsForChristmas.com. We are always posting new, helpful lists.

25 Gifts for Christmas

THE GIFT OF

Your Story

1
The Gift of Your Story

One of the greatest gifts you have is the gift of YOU. It is that gift of YOU that shows up for the rest of the world to see, and it is shown through your own story—through the steps in life you've taken so far. What you have to say shows up in what you do, the way you show up right now, and it shows in the joy and sense of purpose with which you move your story forward.

Your story is the story of a journey. All our stories are. Every step in it counts. Every step is a gift—even the ones that hurt you or maybe even caused pain to your loved ones.

Each step happens in a single moment, and each presents an opportunity to say "yes" to love and "no" to fear and destructive behavior. God speaks to us when we are willing to listen to that voice deep within our soul.

This Advent season, you are discovering the gifts that make up your story. At Christmas, you will present them to Emmanuel, or "God with us." You don't actually have to wait until Christmas, but it's good to take this as a process, as a journey, so you can really soak in each particular gift.

Like all good stories, each of our stories will have ups and downs, and conflicts and resolutions. They will feature heroes and villains or those who challenge us. There will be a love interest as well as pain and passion that come with that love, and, finally, there will be side characters and comic reliefs.

Reflect on your story so far and write down three things for which you are most grateful. Is it the failures or the successes? Maybe what you remember are the people who make your story exciting and challenging.

Finally, ask yourself, "What can I do today to move my story in a direction that will bring me closer to that place where love, and Christ, is born for me?"

THE GIFT OF
Simplicity

2
The Gift of Simplicity

I find it fascinating that the more we understand something complex, the simpler it appears. At the core of the most complicated concept, challenge, or problem, there often lies a solution so simple it makes us laugh or leaves us speechless.

I liken it to a child working through a difficult math problem, and, when they finally 'get it,' they exclaim, "Of course! It's so simple!"

It's like listening to music and being moved by the simplest melody that emerges from the many layers of an intricate arrangement.

Or it's spending a lifetime talking about God, discussing, even arguing about who God really is, only to then find God in the silence of our hearts.

In her book *The Top Five Regrets of the Dying*, Bronnie Ware tells us that most dying people regret not doing more of the simplest things, such as allowing themselves to be happier, staying in touch with friends, having the courage to express their feelings, or not working so hard. Their No. 1 regret? It's the one that I'm sure resonates with many of us—not living truer to who we are instead of what others expect us to be.

The "stuff" we own; the statuses we feel pressured to keep; the social schedules that leave us exhausted. . . . What would happen if, in place of all that, we focused on simplicity?

I once heard from a great spiritual teacher that the reason humans love to complicate things is because doing so builds up their ego and engages their brain. Meanwhile, the heart knows that the Truth is actually very, very simple. The simplicity of how Jesus was born only proves that.

It would be pretty difficult—and unrealistic—to try to change how we live our lives. That's because of how much we depend on technology and different systems, both political and cultural. Instead of feeling bad for not living a simpler life, let's focus on the gifts of simplicity we already do have—gifts that we love and on which we can focus.

What are the three simple things in your life for which you are grateful?

Is it the moment of silence you have before you fall asleep at night? How about hugs with your child before he or she leaves for school? Is it taking that first sip of your morning coffee or tea? Is it just feeling healthy and energized?

Write down your three things (use the downloaded Gratitude Tree) and then reflect on this: What are some areas in your life where you could make more space for simple things—such as being yourself more, expressing your feelings with courage, or keeping in touch with friends? After all, no one likes the thought of the regret that comes with not enjoying the simple things that make life precious.

By the way, a gently used item wrapped in simple brown paper with a bow and a message of love makes a great Christmas present.

THE GIFT OF
Creativity

3
The Gift of Creativity

Have you ever noticed that the words 'Creating' and 'Reacting' have all the same letters? The difference is in where the 'c' is placed. One is in the front; the other tucked in the middle.

We can go through life reacting to situations, places, and people around us; or, we can take part in creating possibilities and opportunities—for ourselves and for those around us.

When we talk about the Gift of Creativity, usually we think about artistic creativity: painting, sculpting, drawing, writing music, singing, dancing. But that is pretty limiting and an uncreative way to think about the amazing gift that creativity is, a gift that each of us possesses.

Right now, during this Advent season, you are creating memories. Undoubtedly, you are being very creative in terms of scheduling all your tasks, errands, family time, and work. If you aren't using your gift of creativity, you are probably in a reactive mode. If so, you are feeling a bit overwhelmed by everything that's going on in your life at this busy time of the year.

By being made in the image and likeness of God, we are made with the gift of creativity. As one of my favorite poets, Maya Angelou, said, "Everybody born comes from the Creator trailing wisps of glory. We come from the Creator with creativity."

We partake in creating life, not only as parents, but also when we decide—regardless of our circumstances—to create a life filled with love, gratitude, and awareness of God's presence. Otherwise, we end up spending too much time reacting to what's around us with fear, anger, resentment, blame, or judgment.

How do you use your gift of Creativity? What are three creative gifts you have that you are most grateful for? Write them down on your Gratitude Tree.

Reflect on those questions above. If you are up for an extra challenge, think of some creative gifts you can give away this Christmas.

THE GIFT OF *Freedom*

4
The Gift of Freedom

Much has been said, written, and sung about the Gift of Freedom. It's the most basic human need, right, and desire.

Since the beginning of time, people have been fighting and dying for freedom. But can true freedom be taken away by outside circumstances? Can someone still feel a lack of freedom in a country that grants everyone the basic freedoms of speech, assembly, and religion as well as the freedom to choose where they live, what kind of work they do, and to make money and spend it as they wish?

I think about the Gift of Freedom every time I enter the women's prison where I mentor inmates. I think about it as I wait for the heavy, impermeable doors to open and let me out. How is this physical prison different from the prisons in which we put ourselves? And what can we do for the people who are imprisoned by addictions, poverty, or lack of opportunities?

Artist Rachel Wolchin says, "Before the truth can set you free, you need to recognize which lie is holding you hostage."

What can the Gift of Freedom bring to you this Advent season?

Can the Gift of Freedom help you to unpack some of the lies about yourself that you have learned to believe? Can you identify the prisons in which you reside?

One of my biggest challenges used to be feeling free to be me. For the longest time I couldn't get there. I didn't feel free to say what I believed without fearing that someone would yell at me, or point their finger at me and publicly humiliate me. This fear was robbing me of my freedom. The lie that someone could truly hurt me with their opinion was holding me hostage. Yes, they could hurt my feelings and damage my ego, but that was a small price to pay for being free.

Can you think of one thing that's holding YOU back from truly living with the Gift of Freedom?

After you have reflected on this for a few minutes, turn your attention to the gifts of freedom you ARE already enjoying, and focus on those. Write down three things that the Gift of Freedom brings to you. It could be that you are grateful for the freedom to sing Christmas songs without being censored. Or for feeling free to dance when no one is watching . . . OR when everyone IS watching.

Perhaps this Christmas you can gift someone with their own Gift of Freedom. When we listen without judgment, we give the freedom of expression.

When we connect in the Core Love with someone of a different religious background, we give the freedom of religion.

When we help someone with a job opportunity, or we create a job for someone, we give the gift of economic freedom.

Thank you for accepting your Gift of Freedom, and, by doing it, helping others to do the same.

THE GIFT OF *Home*

5
The Gift of Home

The first thought that comes to mind when we talk about 'home' is that classic quote you can find on every imaginable decorating object: "Home is where the heart is."

Most of us prefer to live indoors, so we put our heart into that dwelling, whether it's an apartment, a condo, or a house; whether it's small or large; and whether it's crowded or quiet—and make it our 'home.'

Open the Gift of your Home to a stranger this Advent and Christmas season. Invite someone in that you haven't invited in before. Know this: the 'home' you will open to them will be more than just your house itself.

For me, sharing these gifts with you is like visiting with one another in a special room of our shared home—the heart of God. This is where we are safe, together, and connected in our blessings.

For today's reflection, I'd like to borrow the beautiful words of Lebanese-American artist, poet, and writer Kahlil Gibran (from his book *The Prophet*):

"And tell me, people, what have you in these houses? And what is it you guard with fastened doors?

Have you peace, the quiet urge that reveals your power?

Have you remembrances, the glimmering arches that span the summits of the mind?

Have you beauty, that leads the heart from things fashioned of wood and stone to the holy mountain?

Tell me, have you these in your houses?

Or have you only comfort, and the lust for comfort, that stealthy thing that enters the house a guest, and then becomes a host and then a master?

But . . . your house shall be not an anchor but a mast.

It shall not be a glistening film that covers a wound, but an eyelid that guards the eye.

You shall not fold your wings that you may pass through doors, nor bend your heads that they strike not against a ceiling, nor fear to breathe, lest walls should crack and fall down.

You shall not dwell in tombs made by the dead for the living.

And though of magnificence and splendor, your house shall not hold your secret nor shelter your longing.

For that which is boundless in you abides in the mansion of the sky, whose door is the morning mist, and whose windows are the songs and the silences of night."

What are the three things for which you are most grateful concerning the Gift of your Home? As you reflect on those, ponder also if, at times, you see your house, your dwelling, as the "master of you, an anchor that weighs you down" . . . and how you can make it more like a mast that provides a place where you rest, and get restored, allowing you to reach out to others, spreading the gift of your true home where we all are one family.

THE GIFT OF
Family and Loved Ones

6
The Gift of Family and Loved Ones

It was the most natural thing for God to come to us as a child, born into a family.

Perhaps this is the easiest way for God to enter our hearts, since, for most of us, family is where we first experience this unconditional love.

Emmanuel means "God with us," here and present, loving us deeply and unconditionally. Of course, to experience this Love, we must show up fully present, too.

It's the same with our family and loved ones: to both love them and to feel loved by them, we must be present to each other.

Our busy, rushed lives often prevent us from spending more time visiting those we love, even if it means sitting in silence and simply cherishing each other's presence.

At times, there is nothing much we can do about it. Many of us live continents apart from our families; many of us are working two jobs to pay even the most basic bills and can't take the time. Yet, there is something we can do to enjoy this Gift of Family and Loved Ones more, and that is to be more present in those rare moments we DO have.

Have you ever observed a child who wants his mother to pick him up? He isn't thinking about anything else at that moment; his only intention and focus is to get into his mother's arms. The child's natural need to be nurtured and safe is helping him be fully present.

It's a bit different for the parent. How many times did I take one of my children into my arms while talking to a friend or my husband? I didn't pause and give them my full presence. But when I did, time seemed to stop, and I'd feel like the whole universe had paused so my child and I could enjoy the love of one another.

You can do this with a family member or a loved one. Simply bring your awareness into the singular task of loving them, paying attention to them, listening to them, or holding their hand—simply being present.

Reflect on this and then write down three things you're most grateful for that the Gift of Family and Loved Ones brings to you. And next time you have a chance to be with them, give them this gift of your presence.

THE GIFT OF
Uniqueness

7
The Gift of Uniqueness

"Today you are you, that is truer than true. There is no one alive who is youer than you."
— Dr. Seuss

Look at your hands. Look at how uniquely different your fingers are. Look closely at all the different lines on the palms of your hands. There is no one on earth now or ever that has or had the exact same lines as yours.

When you think about the color of your skin, your hair, your eyes, the size and shape of your nose, your features, your body shape, what is the one thing that makes you most unique?

Now, close your eyes and, this time, think about that one gift that you have *inside* of you that makes you unique. This is something you are good at or passionate about—or both—whether you are using this gift or if it's something you aren't sure about yet.

Is it your curiosity, or could it be your optimism? Is it your faith? How about your generosity?

Now think of something inside of you that makes you smile. Perhaps it's your love for watching cute cat videos or your ability to make scrumptious cupcakes.

Next, think of an experience you've gone through that caused you pain, but which also helped you to grow and become the person you are right now.

Do you have anything that others would call a weakness? If so, can you see how you could turn it around and make it a strength? For example, I once coached a woman who hated being strong-willed; as a child she was told she was impossible to manage. Through some inner work, she realized that her strong will was exactly what had helped her to accomplish great things. It created opportunities for her to give back and support others.

Your strengths, your pain, your joys, all your life's experiences, your natural affinities for certain things and activities, your capacity to love, to serve, to give back, to create—and so much more—comprise the uniqueness that no one else on earth has.

All of this, and so much more, is why no one is "youer" than you, as Dr. Seuss says.

Your uniqueness—the very combination of all that makes up the beautiful YOU—Is exactly what the world needs at this point in history. None of us are here by mistake.

Now, write down three unique things about you for which you are most grateful.

And then, take some time to celebrate the unique YOU today.

THE GIFT OF
Compassion

8
The Gift of Compassion

Compassion is a beautiful gift that fuels our desire to make a difference. It often motivates our work. It is the very power behind our willingness to give more, to love deeper, and to bring healing to those in pain.

During this special time of the year, people are more willing to let the Gift of Compassion guide their actions. It inspires us to raise money for the poor and make food for the homeless.

By whatever method you are choosing to give a little extra, know that it is appreciated even if you don't receive a special thank-you card in return. When you give with compassion, the compassion you feel becomes a gift and a reward for YOU.

That's how I came to understand how this gift helps me, when I feel it for others.

Without the Gift of Compassion, we often end up being too hard on ourselves. We look at our suffering as a failure. "How could I get this low?" we ask. "What's wrong with me? I have everything, and I am still making these mistakes that cause me suffering" . . . or "I am such a failure." It's impossible to feel compassion with all this judgment.

The word 'compassion' comes from two Latin words: com ("together") + pati ("to suffer"), or "suffering together."

That explains it. We need someone else with whom we can suffer together. We can't suffer together by ourselves. That's why it's so hard to have compassion for ourselves.

Knowing that God is a compassionate God who understands our suffering and has a desire to alleviate it is the only way to feel compassion for our own suffering and pain. Only then can we let go of the hardness, judgment, guilt, and sense of failure.

When we are compassionate with others, we activate this 'knowing' that God is compassionate with us; we recognize it, and we allow this Gift to flow through us, healing us in the process.

So, what are three things you are grateful for that the Gift of Compassion brings to you? For example, I feel strong compassion for abused women. I want to help them heal. The gift of feeling compassionate brings love into my heart, which in turn heals my own wounds caused by abuse.

As you reflect on the Gift of Compassion, I want to thank YOU for sharing this gift with the world.

THE GIFT OF

Forgiveness

9
The Gift of Forgiveness

I'd like to open this gift by reflecting on these words by Gandhi: "The weak can never forgive. Forgiveness is the attribute of the strong."

As Jesus said, we must forgive seventy times seven, and that requires strength.

There are times that everything in our mind, body, and heart rebels against forgiving another person. When we get hurt, we scream, "No, I will never forgive!" Yet, in our soul, we know we must forgive.

If a friend has broken your trust, or if a spouse has broken the promise of faithful love, is it possible to forgive him or her? Our ego and our heart get wounded; of course, we don't want to forgive. Forgiving also means rebuilding the trust and making ourselves vulnerable to be hurt again.

But coming apart is the only way to heal and be put back together, each time a little bit stronger.

Clemmie Greenlee, a sex-trafficking survivor and founder of Nashville Peacemakers, lost her son to murder. She made it her mission to find the mother of her son's murderer and the boy who killed her son and to forgive them. She knew she had to do that in order to heal.

When I first heard Clemmie's story, I didn't understand how such forgiveness was possible. He was her only son. After many years of being apart, she finally got a chance to be present in his life, only for someone to take him away with one pull of a trigger.

When I met Clemmie, she told me that she wanted to help her son's murderer and his mother first. "I knew if I helped them, I could help myself," Clemmie told me. She knew that the only way she could go on living with love and peace in her heart, and not hatred and anger, was to forgive them and love on them despite the pain they caused her.

What are the three things that Forgiveness has brought into your life for which you are most grateful? Write them down.

Here is an extra challenge: give yourself a Gift of Forgiveness this season. Choose to forgive someone who deeply hurt you.

I know it's hard. I know it seems impossible. But like Clemmie, you can do it. Her compassion and love led her to grant forgiveness. It can do the same for you.

Think of someone you must forgive with that same compassion. Feel LOVE for them, the love that surpasses all understanding and that can't be rationalized. And then see what happens.

THE GIFT OF
Surrender

10
The Gift of Surrender

Who were you before the world told you who you should be? Do you remember yourself when you were fearless, when you were following a dream that you knew was your special mission?

Do you remember how it felt following that dream, when grownups smiled at you in disbelief and you smiled right back, feeling sorry for them because they obviously didn't get it anymore? This is the Gift of Surrender.

When you were a child, it was easy to surrender to God's will, the purpose of your life that simply wanted to fulfill itself. You didn't have to think about how your dream, your purpose, would look like in practical terms. It didn't matter.

Then the doubts and fears came. That is when you learned to rely more on your knowledge and your reason than on your heart. You learned that it's foolish to listen to what's within, and that you had better listen to people around you with their lofty degrees and who "definitely" knew about your destiny and your path much better than you did, or that God did.

You are trapped: you listen to the definitions of success created and proclaimed by the media or the culture we live in—in this tiny sliver of time that comprises a blip in the history of all life—and you accept that as your path.

At this point, you don't even know what "surrender to God's will" would feel like anymore.

It happens to all of us. We spend our whole life searching for the way back to this so-called

"God's will" for our life. We search for that Gift of Surrender: that which would liberate us and heal us from fear; that which would make every minute of our lives a blessing.

We still find glimpses of it in the tiniest moments—like in our lover's kiss when we are willing to build a future together, or when we're holding our newborn baby in our arms, not really knowing what lies ahead, or when we are faced with a challenge and we exhaust all our "reasonable" options. "God, it's your turn now," I say so many times.

When we do surrender, courageously listening to the voice deep within our soul, while rejecting other people's definitions or expectations of us, we are amazed at the doors that open and the paths that appear before us.

What does the Gift of Surrender look like for you? When do you feel most "surrendered"?

Reflect on this . . . and then write down three things for which you are most grateful that occur when you surrender. Use your Gratitude Tree poster.

Now, rest in knowing that the Gift of Surrender to God's love will lead you right into God's arms—just like the Star led the shepherds to the manger, where Jesus was born.

THE GIFT OF *Health*

11
The Gift of Health

Ah, the Gift of Health!

Such a great gift to enjoy this season. I pray that this gift immediately touches those of you who might be suffering from an illness . . . I also pray that this gift touches all of you going forward, whether you happen to be ill now or are as healthy as a horse, as they say.

Imagine if you could open this gift as you wake up every day of your life.

Imagine waking up every day with the gift of health—of feeling good, energized, pain-free . . . and realizing just how precious this gift is. You jump for joy and thank God and the heavens and the angels and the whole universe for it! Imagine that.

And on those days when your body is hurting and you aren't feeling well? That's when you wish you had the Gift of Health more than anything else in the world, right? Do you promise you will take better care of your body and cherish the Gift of Health more, once you get it back? I do.

Some years ago, I was on a concert tour, and on my day off I visited a small gift shop in an upscale town somewhere in America. It had been a particularly challenging stretch of concerts in an area where traffic was bad, rents and mortgages were high, the cost of living was incredibly expensive, and time was a luxury. At the time it seemed to me that very few people there could honor the Gift of Health and keep it.

Immersed in thoughts and prayers for our rushed, difficult world and the people in it, I walked into the shop and noticed a sign on the wall with these words from Dalai Lama imprinted on it:

"Man surprised me most about humanity. Because he sacrifices his health in order to make money. Then he sacrifices money to recuperate his health. . . . He lives as if he is never going to die, and then dies having never really lived."

It's easy to get too busy during Christmas season to take care of our health. The sugary treats don't help either. Without the Gift of Health, we can't make new memories and honor all the traditions that keep us busy.

So, pause today, and reflect on just how precious this Gift of Health is to you. Write down three words that best express your gratitude for this gift. For example, my three words are walking, sleeping, and fruits and vegetables. OK, that's four. When I walk, go to sleep, and eat fruits and vegetables, I say a prayer of gratitude for my health.

Keep the awareness of this gift throughout this season, and beyond. It is a precious gift.

THE GIFT OF
Courage

12
The Gift of Courage

When I first moved to Tennessee, I started noticing this one quote by Joyce Meyer everywhere—in coffee shops, doctor's offices, gas stations: "Courage is fear that has said its prayers and decided to go forward anyway."

Living in the South, I also see this one: "Courage is being scared to death . . . and saddling up anyway," by John Wayne.

I think of Mary, mother of Jesus, as a courageous woman. She said "Yes" to God, to giving birth to the Messiah! She did this even though she was just a teenager, unwed at the time and knowing that she might be stoned to death.

It's also quite easy to see the gift of courage in the lives of people such as Joan of Arc, Rosa Parks, or Nelson Mandela.

But there is even more to the Gift of Courage. Author and researcher Brene Brown points out that the root of the word 'courage' is *cor*, the Latin word for 'heart.' In one of its earliest forms, the word 'courage' meant. "To speak one's mind by telling all one's heart."

It takes courage to speak honestly and openly about our deepest secrets and experiences, both good and bad.

I meet many women and men at my speaking engagements and concert tours who, encouraged by hearing stories of overcoming fear and healing, share with me their own difficult stories: stories of addictions, broken relationships, abuse . . . some of them opening up about it for the first time in their lives.

What has the Gift of Courage brought into your life that you are most grateful for? For me, it's freedom. When I chose courage over fear of rejection or judgment, I felt free because I no longer had to hide past experiences that had caused me so much shame and pain.

Can you find the courage to say "Yes" like Mary did? Can you step out of your comfort zone and make space in your heart to receive more love, more grace, and more truth, in the process courageously trusting God's guidance?

Reflect on this, and remember that the root of 'courage' is *cor*, your heart.

THE GIFT OF *Journey*

13
The Gift of Journey

Imagine if our lives were stuck in one spot. Like an old, vinyl record stuck on a phrase that keeps repeating. Or like sitting in a rocking chair, feeling the sensation of moving, but staying in the same place. Or going around and around on a carousel and never getting anywhere.

Luckily, life is not like that. Rather, it's a journey. Being aware of this Gift of Journey throughout our lives makes it especially rewarding.

Our big life journey through time takes us from our first breath to our last breath, constantly moving forward like a river. On that journey we travel through different places. While we are making that outward journey, we also make another one that matters even more and is as adventurous—the journey inward.

For thirteen years I traveled around America with my family--my husband and our three sons. We crossed the continent many times and lost count of the mileage we covered. We saw many different places: small towns, big cities, mountains, plains, and oceans. We moved fast and watched the scenery change before our eyes. But the real change we experienced happened on the inside, between the trips. That's when we sat still and took time to process all that we had learned, the people we had encountered, the things we had uncovered about ourselves.

The journey inward is, in a way, a journey to Bethlehem. To the birthplace of Emmanuel— "God with us." If we never journey inward to find God, we'll wander around like orphans, always looking for another path to take and never being satisfied.

Take some time today to sit still and use the Gift of Journey inward. Then ask yourself, "What are three things that journeying has brought to the surface for me—and helped me understand them . . . or heal them?" It could be some painful memory that you need to grieve through and release, or it could be a dream that God put into your heart and which you had forgotten about.

Reflect on this, write your three thoughts on your Gratitude Tree, and continue the journey toward the place where Jesus was born for you.

THE GIFT OF *Joy*

14
The Gift of Joy

Open the Gift of Joy today. Not just the feeling of great pleasure and happiness, as 'joy' is defined in the dictionary, but the joy that we feel AND know deep within.

Early on in my journey of faith, I got to play Mary in *The Miracle of Christmas*, a musical produced by a big Christian theatre on the East Coast. As I prepared for the role and did an in-depth character study, I gained all kinds of insight into Mary and what her experience might have felt like.

I remember vividly the moment I sang "Magnificat" on the opening night. It was set up as a duet with Elizabeth (Mary's cousin and the mother of John the Baptist).

The actress portraying Elizabeth and I held hands while we sang Mary's words: "My soul magnifies the Lord and my spirit rejoices in God my savior." I felt as if I needed the physical touch to keep me grounded, because the joy of the moment was overwhelming.

I remember writing in my acting journal: "The Joy Mary must have felt about giving birth to God's son was like knowing without a doubt that there is a cure for cancer and that all the people you love now would be healed. The joy so big and so overwhelming that all of you disappears gladly with gratitude and humility and honor—completely surrendered and given to the Greatness of God."

It's the joy so big, it cancels out all pain, all fear, all doubt, all darkness.

When I experience even a tiny fraction of that Joy, I can't stop singing, either. I dance, I laugh, I scream, I give thanks, I hold hands and give hugs and stand tall with my arms wide open, and breathe deep and know I am a part of something much bigger than me.

Can you tap into that Joy today, this Advent season? Can you imagine yourself in Mary's shoes? Can you for a moment try to feel what she was feeling? Perhaps read the words of "Magnificat" out loud, or put on "Joy to the World," turn up the volume, and sing along.

And then, when the Joy passes through you, take some time to be still, and reflect. Think about three things that you have every day that could bring you that same joy. Like your children, or your puppy, or the sun in the sky, or the moment in which—with full presence of mind and heart—you receive Christ.

Write down these three things so you can always be reminded of the Gift of Joy.

15
The Gift of Music

I am quite partial to the Gift of Music!

To me, music has always been a connection to the Divine. When I was little, it's how I knew there was more to what we can see and touch and explain.

Music is like magic. It can transport us to where we want to be, feel what we want to feel, or connect us with strangers across the globe.

Music helps our brain to learn and to pay attention. It improves memory, helps us express our feelings, and has always been a form of communication.

Christmas season is such a great opportunity to participate in this Gift of Music and sing together. After years and years of hearing "Jingle Bells" and "Santa Claus Is Coming to Town" and "Silent Night," everyone surely knows the words. And yet so many people say, "I can't sing."

I often tell them, that's just like saying, "I can't run." If you don't practice singing, you can certainly forget how to do it and become insecure. We just don't sing enough.

At our house parties, we always gather around the piano, ask our guests to pull up lyrics of songs on their smartphones and sing along. Then no one has an excuse that they don't know the words.

Of course, the Gift of Music is also very powerful and healing when we just listen with an open heart and open mind. This is the time to let our soul resonate with sound waves and all the invisible, divine particles that travel along them.

Our brains are wired in a way that connects music with long-term memory. Songs can pull up the memory of our deepest emotions and help us to heal.

On Christmas Eve, when my children are asleep, I sit at my piano and play "Silent Night," one note at a time. I listen to the vibrations, the overtones, and the silence between two notes. It is there that I find peace, joy, love, and sometimes sadness and loneliness for those who are no longer with me. There, in the Gift of Music, my soul connects with the Divine, and I experience Christmas all over again.

What does the Gift of Music bring to you? Can you think of three instances that make you grateful for music? For example, when I sing, I am able to release tears and stubborn pain, and for that I am grateful. Or when we have a hard time falling asleep, I am grateful for lullabies.

If you are insecure about your singing, do this: write down a list of three songs that you know how to sing—songs like "You Are My Sunshine" or "Tis a Gift to Be Simple"—and sing them every day. See what happens in a few weeks.

THE GIFT OF
Dance

16
The Gift of Dance

When was the last time you danced? Twirled and moved your body, laughing and running out of breath, and getting dizzy from spinning? Do you remember how good it felt to dance?

I hope many of you reading or listening are saying, "Oh, I dance every morning. Just to get my blood moving and my heart smiling."

Most of us think we must go somewhere to dance . . . that we must dress up, take lessons, practice. No, we don't. Dancing is so natural to us that even if we have given up dancing, our bodies never do.

Jamie Marich, who I interviewed on *Waking Up in America,* is a clinical counselor specializing in trauma. She founded Dancing Mindfulness in which she uses the Gift of Dance in the healing process.

When I worked on our episode, I became more aware how much I sway when I stand, tap my feet, or move my hands while I talk. She pointed out to me that our bodies naturally want to move in this rhythm of life, creating a physical movement that unlocks the movement of pain or anxiety that we hold in.

"Dance . . . is a river . . . it takes us to that journey where we need to go for healing . . . [it's] responding to the needs of the body," Jamie says.

David danced before the Lord, and the Psalmists called us to praise God's name with dancing. We were told that there was a time to weep and a time to laugh; a time to mourn and a time to dance.

When is your time to dance? What happens to your body when you do dance? Can you recognize what the Gift of Dance brings into your life? Write down three of those blessings on your Gratitude Tree or in your journal.

As you work this Advent season, bake in your kitchen, walk down the busy streets while shopping, or even as you sit in front of your computer ordering gifts online, observe how your body is moving. If you are tapping a foot, stand up, follow the rhythm, and dance. If you feel restless, move your body in long, slow motions. Dance to the music of your life . . . it doesn't even have to be songs. Listen to your body's cues and dance.

And reflect on this:

"I danced in the morning when the world was young.
I danced in the moon and the stars and the sun.
I came down from heaven and I danced on the earth.
At Bethlehem, I had my birth.

Dance, dance, wherever you may be.
I am the lord of the dance, said he.
And I lead you all, wherever you may be.
And I lead you all in the dance, said he."

(Words by Sydney Carter set to the tune of an American Shaker song "Simple Gifts")

THE GIFT OF
Fragrance

17
The Gift of Fragrance

The Gift of Fragrance is one gift that, much like music, has the power to transport us—to our childhood, to the family kitchen, to a vacation spot, or to someplace less pleasant, such as a hospital or a dentist's waiting room.

My children recognize Sundays by the fragrance of a specific homemade meal. Thanksgiving begins the moment that the apples and cranberries start simmering on the stove. Christmas is accompanied by the fragrances of pine needles, hot chocolate, or warmed-up wine spiced with cloves, cinnamon sticks, and star anise.

But no two people smell things the same way. Depending on our genome, the receptors that are activated by the same smell can be very different from one person to the next.

So, the Gift of Fragrance is a very personal experience—both in how we receive it and what we find in it, as well as what it connects us with.

I think one of the most beautiful prayers ever written is the "Fragrance Prayer" by Mother Teresa that starts with the line: "Dear Jesus, help me to spread Your fragrance everywhere I go."

What does that mean for you?

What is the fragrance of Jesus? Of Love, Light, Life, Hope, Healing?

I know that however you identify it, it will be very personal, and it can never be bottled up and sold at the fragrance counter.

Reflect on this today, and then write down your thoughts on three things that the Gift of Fragrance has brought into your life or the lives of others. For example, I am grateful for the Gift of Fragrance because it helps bring my awareness into the present moment.

The soothing fragrance of lavender oil helps me relax at night. The fragrance of incense and my lavender soy candle made by the women of Thistle Farms—survivors of sex trafficking, addiction, and abuse—remind me of life's challenges and the never-failing truth that Love Heals.

What does the fragrance of Christmas, of Love, look like, smell like, feel like for you?

THE GIFT OF
Breaking Bread

18
The Gift of Breaking Bread

Today's gift is something most of us give thanks for every day—the Gift of Breaking Bread. This is the food that sustains us; it is the food that we grow, prepare, and share with others—friends and strangers alike.

Because bread is such a basic gift that's just another line on our grocery list instead of the treasured and cherished gift it should be, let's spend some time in reflection and gratitude.

Dealing with bread was one of the big adjustments I had to make when I moved to America. Growing up in Croatia, buying bread had been a daily task. Bakeries would deliver fresh bread to the stores in the morning, and we would go buy only as much as was needed for that day. Half of a kilo loaf would be enough for our family of five.

And we served bread with everything! I often try to remember how this was possible. The only explanation I can come up with is that it wasn't the quantity of bread that fed us, but how we ate it. We shared it conscientiously, savoring every bite with gratitude.

I never quite got used to buying bagged bread in America. I still buy fresh bread most days.

Breaking bread is also a sacred ritual; for many Christians, it represents a communion with God. For others, it's an extension of friendship, connection, care, and respect; it's a symbol of welcoming someone into your home, to your table, and into your heart.

What do you find most precious in the Gift of Breaking Bread? What can you do this

Christmas to open up your home and your heart even wider and let strangers know they are welcome to partake in the holy feast?

What are three things you are most grateful for concerning the Gift of Breaking Bread? Write them down. As you enjoy your meal today, say an extra prayer for those who are lonely, rejected, judged, abandoned, hungry, poor, and forgotten. May God and Love lead us all to an open table where the heavenly food awaits us.

THE GIFT OF *Time*

19
The Gift of Time

Here is one Gift each of us is given at birth and so many regret they didn't spend it better: the Gift of Time.

"Don't say you don't have enough time. You have exactly the same number of hours per day that were given to Helen Keller, Pasteur, Michaelangelo, Mother Teresa, Leonardo da Vinci, Thomas Jefferson, and Albert Einstein."

I love this quote by author H. Jackson Brown Jr. about having the same number of hours per day given to everyone else. Even though, sometimes, it surely doesn't feel like it.

Time is a funny thing. Although it's a constant for everyone, some people seem to "have" more of it than others. And sometimes it's influenced by what's happening around us.

I have a friend, a Franciscan nun, who moved from a quiet village in the mountains of Bosnia and Herz to New York City. Her job was to cook for the community. Back home she fed three times as many people, but one day she told me, "I don't know what is happening. I have the same schedule, cook for fewer people, but time flies so much faster; here, I always feel rushed."

Yes, for all of us, sometimes the time flies and sometimes, like on a long flight, it seems to drag.

One thing is for sure: the only time we have is NOW. This moment . . . and this . . . and now this one. It's how we are present in this moment that makes it go slower or faster, unappreciated or cherished. We don't get Time back. We can get compensated for the lost time, but we can't ever get it back. So, it's important that each moment is lived fully.

That's true for even the moments in which it feels like other people or circumstances beyond our control are wasting our time . . . like being stuck in traffic.

Or sitting at the airport because our flight has been delayed or cancelled. Or the hours we spend doing something we don't like doing; that drains us.

Do you get resentful and/or grumpy at those times? Or are you able to say: "This is the only time I get. I'll be present in it no matter how hard, dull, or even painful it is."

What does "time well spent" look like for you?

Is it with your family and loved ones? Is it reading and learning?

What about sacred time? That's the time of "Be Still and Know I Am God." It's refreshing, renewing, and life-giving for me.

Where are you on your timeline right now? How are you spending the Gift of Time you have been given?

What are the three things you are most grateful for that the Gift of Time made possible for you?

One thing I am grateful for is the time I lost being stuck in the past, so today I know the Gift of Time is in being present.

Now, reflect on the Gift of Time and write. And take your time doing it.

THE GIFT OF
Silence

20
The Gift of Silence

Today's gift, Silence, might seem a rarity in the world we live in. But no matter how much noise we humans make, silence will always be there in the background and in the spaces in between. No matter how hard we try to escape it, silence is waiting for us. And it's easier to access it than we realize.

We need silence. We need it to rest, to heal, to sort out our thoughts and feelings, to listen for the whisper deep within our soul for guidance. And yet, we try hard to fill every moment with noise and distractions.

In fact, for those of you listening to this, I'm going to fade out the music and let silence be our backdrop.

For many, silence can be uncomfortable, awkward, unpleasant. In silence we are much more likely to hear the truths about ourselves and about our lives—the stuff we'd rather not think about.

In my early twenties, when I was first learning how to pray, I asked a Franciscan priest how to enter into this deep silence. I wanted to learn the contemplative prayer because I had so much stuff I had to work through: grief, broken trust, fear, sense of self, and so on. I lived in the heart of Manhattan at the time, where the noise never stops. I knew that my sense of peace, calm, and sanity depended on finding silence.

The priest taught me how to access silence at any time by going inward and silencing my own thoughts first.

It took me a long time to be able to do this, and I really immersed myself in contemplative prayer. But the process of learning to silence my thoughts did not only bring the silence to me, it also made me pay attention to all kinds of thoughts I had, why I had them, and where they were coming from. I learned a lot about myself through learning how to sit in silence.

When we emerge out of the silence, the music of our lives sounds so much richer, more harmonious, filled with gratitude and joy.

The most beautiful Christmas carol, "Silent Night," was born out of silence—a broken organ, a church without music, and a pastor who took a long walk through the silent hills of Austria.

We wait in silence so we are absolutely ready to hear the whisper of Love when it calls us. The silence opens up the space within our hearts and our minds to receive gifts beyond what our limited human minds can think up.

Reflect on this and ask yourself, "What are three things for which I am most grateful that silence brings to me?"

Spend some time in silence today. And start your own daily practice of silence—contemplative prayer or meditation. See what changes in your life.

THE GIFT OF
Gratitude

21
The Gift of Gratitude

Let me begin today's reflection by congratulating you! Including today, you have opened twenty-one gifts and have practiced gratitude with each of them. If the research is true that it takes a minimum of twenty-one days to develop a habit, you just gave today's gift to yourself—the Gift of Gratitude.

Practicing gratitude offers many benefits. Many studies have been done on this, but even without the scientific research, it's easy to see how being grateful can turn even the hardest of circumstances into a beautiful life.

In a Five-Step Practice to find more joy and purpose that I use in my life and teach in my online course, one of the most important steps is the internal shift, in which the turning point takes place. And one of the most effective triggers of big internal shifts is gratitude.

It's natural for us to feel grateful. And there is always something in our lives, no matter how small, to be thankful for. Since we can't be grateful and resentful at the same time, and it's hard to feel grateful and angry simultaneously, the Gift of Gratitude paves the road to big shifts and deeper happiness.

Gratitude also activates Grace in our lives, as a grateful heart is open and able to receive more.

So, let's continue the Gratitude practice. What are the three things you are most grateful for about the Gift of Gratitude? I can tell you that the biggest one for me is how I feel when I choose gratitude: fulfilled, happy, calm, energized.

Now it's your turn.

And thank you for your willingness to receive these Gifts. Through it you have given me a Gift of Gratitude.

THE GIFT OF
Grace

22
The Gift of Grace

This is one of those gifts that's available to everyone, always. Grace is present in our lives even when we aren't aware of it. Even in our darkest moments, when we can't seem to access it through our own ability or will, the Gift of Grace is there.

Everything about Christmas involves the Gift of Grace. It is there in every moment of it: in the waiting for the Messiah; in the moment when the angel Gabriel spoke to Mary; in the birth of Jesus; and in the journey of the shepherds and three wise men.

The Gift of Grace is present in every gift we have opened or will open in this Advent Calendar, and it is there in every other gift given to us each day.

Grace is available all the time, to all of us.

Reflect on this amazing Gift today.

Think of all the times you've been aware of God's amazing Grace in your life. Perhaps there were some big moments in which you experienced a miracle because of this gift. Or, perhaps it's the moment while you are sipping your morning tea or coffee with gratitude that you are aware of God's Grace.

One of my biggest life challenges is how to string together moments of grace into a grace-filled life; or, more accurately, how to keep my awareness of God's grace in my life—as well as the lives of others—in my every waking moment.

What are you most grateful for that the Gift of Grace brings into your life? Reflect on this, write down three things in big, bold letters, because it is the Gift of Grace that fills every other gift we've been given.

23
The Gift of Light

It's almost Christmas!

We have only three more gifts left to open. Today's gift is the Gift of Light.

In the beginning there was heaven and earth, and the earth was formless and empty and dark. Then God said, "Let there be light," and there was light.

Do you know how good it feels to see the light after being in darkness for a long time?

If you've ever driven through the night, you'd know how amazing it feels to see the first rays of dawn at the break of morning.

If you've ever felt hurt that is so painful that it darkened the sun for you, you'd know how good it feels to feel the light when it returns to your life.

If you've experienced shame or guilt that kept your eyes pointed toward the ground and your heart closed to God's love and forgiveness, you know how life-giving that Light felt on your face once you lifted up your chin.

I love the fact that Christmas in the northern hemisphere is set during the darkest time of the year. I love how we put up millions of little, decorative lights to break up that darkness. I often think how symbolic it is to use the tiny little lights strung together (even though they are terribly inefficient and unreliable). I often think the strings of lights are like people standing together with their hands clasped, some broken, but all ready to shine our lights, doing our best in anticipation of the coming of life-giving Light.

The Gift of Light helps guide us to the place where Jesus is born. It will always guide us from darkness to the place where we can find Love waiting.

The Gift of Light helps us to illuminate the parts of our souls, our hearts, and our minds where we still hang on to stuff we are ashamed of, or which makes us feel guilt.

Today, accept the Gift of Light and let it bore deep within you. Let it shine on all the corners and beneath the proverbial rugs under which we like to sweep our troubles and our secrets. Let it illuminate you completely and lead you to a place of your New Life with Emmanuel—"God with us."

Contemplate on the Gift of Light and what it brings to you—today, this Christmas, and going forward. Write down three things for which you are most grateful, and then sit with your chin up and feel the light shining on your heart.

THE GIFT OF *Life*

24
The Gift of Life

It's Christmas Eve. And today, it's time to open the Gift of Life.

Life is something you are given each moment—through every breath you take. This is true for your physical life and your spiritual life.

How are you spending this Gift? What are you bringing to it?

One year, I was performing my Christmas concert in a busy parish. It was a week before Christmas, and the priest was telling the congregation about how, in our me-oriented world, we tend to think that Christmas is all about us and not about Jesus. Afterward, I asked the priest, "If Christmas is not about me, who is it about? Would God really go through the whole birth thing just for his own sake?"

Imagine standing right next to the manger where God showed up on that night. Imagine knowing that there was no one more important than you to receive the Gift of Life that moment. Because that's how it is.

It is our own false humility, our own sense of brokenness, that stands outside of the stable and on the sidelines saying, "No, not me . . . I surely am not worthy of this great gift of Life . . ." And yet, you have already been given it! It's not up to you to reject the fullness of it, but it is absolutely up to you to jump up and down with joy, like a child opening a gift and finding that it's what he's been wishing for. It's up to you to accept this gift with unreserved gratitude. humility, and honor.

The Gift of Life

This gift IS for you. It is already yours. You are living it, breathing it, thriving in it . . . struggling as you grow and journey through it. This is the Gift of Life, a gift that only God can give.

Reflect on this today, and have a Blessed Christmas Eve!

THE GIFT OF *Love*

25
The Gift of Love

Thank you for opening these 25 Gifts with me. Thank you for opening your heart to receive them, to reflect on all that you already have, and to give thanks for it.

This last gift is the one you can use as a wrapper or as a big gift bag in which you bring all the other gifts and present them to God and to the people in your life—the Gift of Love.

In everything you do, let this Gift be a delivery method. Love is the source of where all the other gifts come from. Everything you and I have been given comes wrapped in this gift.

May this gift be the one you use in everything you do, with every thought you think, and in every decision you make. May you choose the Gift of Love to guide you as you deal with pain, uncertainty, and fear.

May you always stay wide open to receive it, and give it freely without any reservation. Because this Gift of Love will never get entirely spent.

Today, Love is born for you. And you don't have to wait until another Christmas to come to it. It is there waiting for you—the unconditional, nonjudgmental, accepting, comforting, and healing Gift of Love.

Give thanks for it, and have a blessed and Merry Christmas.

Acknowledgments

This book and project would not have happened without the tremendous support of my dear friend, Stephanie Cornett. Stephanie encouraged me every step of the way, read the chapters, reviewed the graphics, and even helped design the cover.

Davor Bozic, a musician and old friend from Slovenia—with whom I sang love duets when we were barely seventeen years old—offered to put some finishing touches and sprinkle some Christmas pixie dust on the audio recordings. I'm deeply grateful and can't wait for another chance to collaborate.

When I thought this project would have to wait another year to see the light of day, Mike Towle appeared and offered his amazing editing and book-consulting skills. I couldn't have hoped to find a better book partner! Thank you!

My husband, Matthew, encouraged me to finish this book and launch it even if it meant stealing our together-hours—as he was battling Stage 4 cancer. You are the biggest, most precious gift I have ever received. I love you forever.

My kids—Dante, Evan, and Blais—have been an endless source of inspiration, wisdom, and motivation for me to see each day as a true blessing.

Finally, my mother, Stefica, provided love, healing, and comfort to me as I worked on this book during my husband's illness. Long before my American Christmases, she taught me the real gifts that Christmas brings. Thank you.

Songs to Enjoy with These Gifts

The Gift of Your Story ("O Come Divine Messiah")

The Gift of Freedom ("O Come O Come Emmanuel")

The Gift of Home ("I'll Be Home for Christmas")

The Gift of Family and Loved Ones ("What Child Is This")

The Gift of Uniqueness ("One Solitary Life")

The Gift of Compassion ("I Failed Again")

The Gift of Forgiveness ("Kyrie Eleison")

The Gift of Health ("How I Love the Christmas Season")

The Gift of Courage ("Breath of Heaven")

The Gift of Journey ("To Bethl'em of Judea")

The Gift of Music ("Gloria in Excelsis Deo")

The Gift of Dance ("Christmas Dance")

The Gift of Breaking Bread ("Panis Angelicus")

The Gift of Silence ("Silent Night")

The Gift of Gratitude ("Ave Maria")

25 GIFTS FOR CHRISTMAS

The Gift of Grace ("Amazing Grace")

The Gift of Life ("Little One")

The Gift of Love ("Merry Christmas")

All songs listed are available for download/purchase at 25GiftsforChristmas.com

Also by Tatiana 'Tajci' Cameron

DVD and CD of Tajci's Christmas special. As seen on major faith channels.

Turning Points - a collection of essays and interviews with guests appearing on *Waking Up in America*.

Available on Amazon.com
and
the Waking UP Store
at WakingUPrevolution.com

About the Author

Tatiana 'Tajci' Cameron is an award-winning music artist and an inspirational speaker who combines music and wellness to coach people through life's transformations. She is a holistic life coach certified through Radiant Health Institute. Her first book, *Turning Points*, was published in 2015.

Tajci was a pop superstar at age nineteen, selling out arenas and achieving platinum status. She also has presented 1,000-plus keynote concerts, produced the TV show *Waking Up in America*, and blogged on HuffPost. Her *Story of Christmas* has been experienced by millions of people through live events and TV broadcasts.

She mentors at the Tennessee State Prison for Women with "Better Decisions" and is an advocate for victims of abuse, rape, and sex trafficking. She cherishes spending Christmas with her husband and their three sons at their Franklin, Tennessee home.

Tajci.net
WakingUPrevolution.com

#wakingUPrevolution

Made in the USA
Lexington, KY
18 November 2019